Suryia Swims!

The True Story of How an Orangutan Learned to Swim

Bhagavan "Doc" ANTLE with Thea FELDMAN

Photographs by Barry BLAND

Henry Holt and Company • New York

Henry Holt and Company, LLC
Publishers since 1866
175 Fifth Avenue, New York, New York 10010
mackids.com

Henry Holt® is a registered trademark of Henry Holt and Company, LLC.
Text copyright © 2012 by Thea Feldman
Photographs copyright © 2012 by Bhagavan Antle

Library of Congress Cataloging-in-Publication Data
Antle, Bhagavan.
Suryia swims! : the true story of how an orangutan
learned to swim / Bhagavan "Doc" Antle, with Thea Feldman ;
photographs by Barry Bland. — 1st ed.
p.   cm.

Summary: Although orangutans are not supposed to like water, an orangutan
living at a wildlife preserve in South Carolina plays with her dog friend in the
bathtub and learns to swim and dive in the pool. Based on a true story.
ISBN 978-0-8050-9317-9 (hc)
1. Orangutan—Juvenile fiction. [1. Orangutan—Fiction. 2. Swimming—
Fiction. 3. Wildlife refuges—Fiction.] I. Feldman, Thea. II. Bland, Barry, ill.
III. Title.
PZ10.3.A63Sv 2012   [E]—dc23   2011029047

First Edition—2012
Designed by Véronique Lefèvre Sweet and Elynn Cohen
Printed in China by Macmillan Production Asia, Ltd., Kwun Tong, Kowloon,
Hong Kong
(Vendor Code: 10)

1 3 5 7 9 10 8 6 4 2

To Suryia—
to your bright mind and big heart
—B. A.

Suryia the orangutan and his best friend, Roscoe the dog, played outdoors all day long. They ran around and rolled on the ground until it was time to go indoors with Suryia's human friend Moksha. Suryia, Roscoe, and Moksha all lived at a wildlife preserve in South Carolina. Many other animals lived there, too.

What did a busy orangutan like Suryia do after a full day of play?

He took a bath!

The bath was Moksha's idea, but Suryia loved to splash around in a tub full of soapy bubbles. Sometimes Suryia took a bath with his orangutan friends. The other orangutans didn't enjoy having a bath as much as Suryia did. That's because most orangutans do not like water.

Most orangutans do not have a dog for a best friend, either. Suryia was different. He even took baths with Roscoe. Roscoe was happy when they were finished. But for Suryia, bath time was still playtime!

Suryia had such a good time in the tub that Moksha decided to bring him to the pool. Suryia watched Moksha swim. Every time she passed Suryia, Moksha reached up and tickled him! Suryia loved this new game.

Many of Suryia's friends swam in the pool, too.
Bubbles the elephant moved gracefully through
the water, leaving behind a trail of . . . bubbles!

Tonks the tiger paddled in the pool on hot summer days.

And little Ondar the baby bear enjoyed taking a dip with Moksha.

Everyone was having such a good time. Suryia liked to have a good time, too! So one day, while Moksha was in the pool, Suryia put his head under the water and looked at her. That was fun! Suryia dunked his head again and again. At first, he put his finger under his nose to keep the water out. But he quickly learned how to hold his breath.

Before long, Suryia went all the way into the pool. He held his breath and moved his arms and legs.

He moved forward in the water.

Suryia was swimming! He was doing something no other orangutan had ever done before—he was swimming just for fun.

Swimming in the pool became one of Suryia's favorite things to do. He was so comfortable in the water that he didn't always need his life vest.

Suryia especially loved to
swim with Moksha. Sometimes
he would hold her hand. And
sometimes he would give her
a big hug in the water!

The pool soon became another fun place where
Suryia and Roscoe often played together.

Suryia also swam a lot with Otty the otter.

He swam with Baku
the tapir, too.

Even a pair of
leopard cubs got their
fur wet with Suryia!

But Suryia had the most fun in the water with the tigers. Tigers just love being in water!

Suryia also learned to dive. He loved to hold his breath and swim down in the water. Moksha would surprise Suryia by putting things for him to play with at the bottom of the pool. He especially liked the pretty plastic rings he sometimes found there.

Suryia was no ordinary orangutan. He liked to try as many new things as possible! That's how he came to have a dog for a best friend. It's how he learned to enjoy the water. And it's how he discovered he could swim and dive. There was no telling what Suryia might do next!

Author's Note

Suryia, Roscoe, and their friends live at a wildlife preserve in Myrtle Beach, South Carolina, called T.I.G.E.R.S. (The Institute for Greatly Endangered and Rare Species), where Suryia learned to swim. Although there have been rare sightings of orangutans getting into water in the wild, there is no evidence of them actually swimming. Their evolutionary history has taught them to beware of dangers, such as crocodiles, that lurk in water. Because of this, the intuition that would have encouraged orangutans to swim never developed.

So what happened at the T.I.G.E.R.S. preserve to reverse that history? Cared for by skilled wildlife professionals such as Moksha Bybee, the animals that live at the preserve enjoy a nurturing and fulfilling life. They are less concerned with survival because their lives are secure and their needs are met. In this comfortable environment, their intellect and curiosity can grow. In addition, Suryia has the opportunity to see examples of other swimming animals at the preserve, which also helped him overcome his natural aversion to water.

Orangutans are highly endangered, primarily because their natural habitats have been destroyed by logging and converted for palm oil cultivation. Buying foods that use palm oil contributes to the destruction of orangutan habitats. Bhagavan "Doc" Antle founded the T.I.G.E.R.S. preserve to provide grassroots support and protection for orangutans and other endangered species. For nearly thirty years, T.I.G.E.R.S. and its parent organization, the Rare Species Fund, have supplied funding, training, and staff to wildlife projects worldwide. Visit RareSpeciesFund.org.

Suryia and Bhagavan Antle